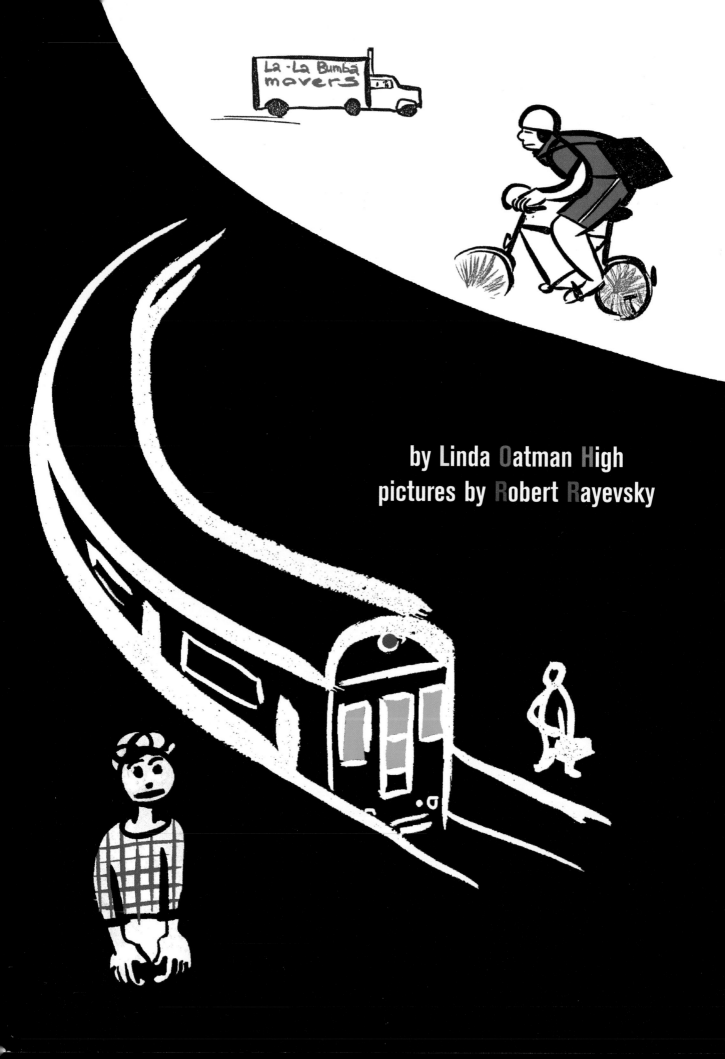

by Linda Oatman High
pictures by Robert Rayevsky

UNDER NEW YORK

above

Holiday House / New York

Library of Congress Cataloging-in-Publication Data
High, Linda Oatman.
Under New York / by Linda Oatman High ; illustrated by Robert Rayevsky.
p.   cm.
ISBN 0-8234-1551-1 (hardcover)
1. New York (N.Y)—Description and travel—Juvenile literature. 2. Underground
areas—New York (State)—New York—Juvenile literature. [1. New York (N.Y.)—
Description and travel. 2. Underground areas.] I. Rayevsky, Robert, ill. II. Title.

F128.33 .H54 2001
974.7'1—dc21   00-039606

10/01 B+T

J
974.71
H

To Zach ><> L.O.H.

To Маня, Кира и Раф.   Папа

Under New York,
below skyscrapers and moonshine and sky,
there are stones and sand, clay, and lots of big rocks
made by glaciers,
millions of years ago.

Under New York,
below taxicabs and tour buses and carriage horses,
there are railroad tracks and trains whizzing past,
clattering fast,
bringing visitors to the city and taking them home again.

Under New York,
below offices and theaters and stores,
there are miles of pipes and wires,
yellow and orange, pink and red and black,
carrying light and heat to the city above.

Under New York,
below sidewalks and manholes and streets,
there are roaring machines and open elevators,
ladders and shafts and workers,
making new tunnels for water.

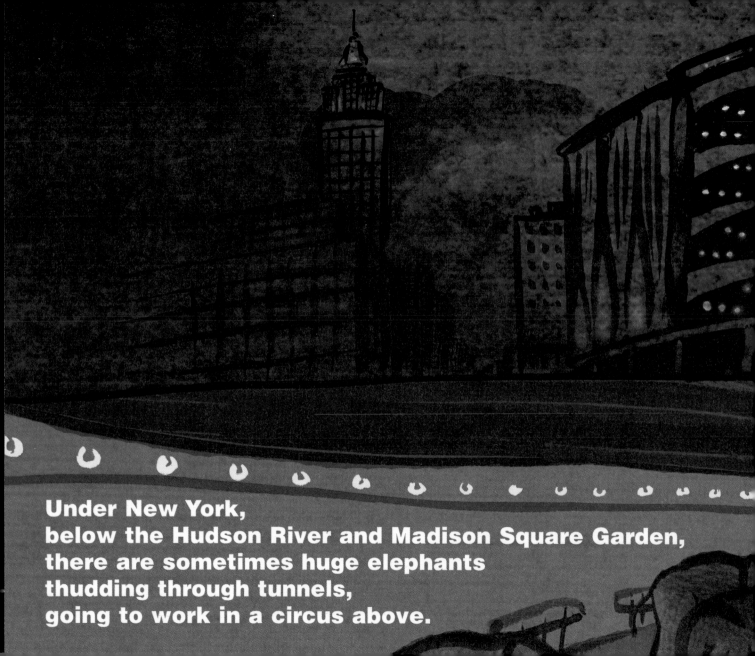

**Under New York,
below the Hudson River and Madison Square Garden,
there are sometimes huge elephants
thudding through tunnels,
going to work in a circus above.**

Under New York,
below pigeons and stray cats and dogs,
there are restaurants and jazz clubs,
shimmering with lights and saxophones of brass.

During off-hours trains stop here

Do not hold doors

Transfer L 1 2 3 9

Please

Under New York,
below garbage and car horns and billboards,
there is a music man in the subway station,
wearing a tuxedo of white,
making beautiful tunes with his violin.

Under New York,
below nighttime and morning and noon,
sun and stars and moon,
there is a world of its own,
an underground city below the city . . .

↗ Exit

Chinese Zodiac Symbols 鼠 rat 牛 ox 虎 tiger 兔 rabbit 龙 dragon 蛇 snake

马 horse　羊 goat　猴 monkey　鸡 rooster　狗 dog　猪 pig

under New York.

SHOW
TONIGHT
at 8:30 p.m.

Subway **Station**
Uptown & Downtown &
Queens Brooklyn

(Some) Notes from Underground

New Yorkers hardly ever think about what is happening beneath their feet – unless something goes wrong. Utilities, such as water pipes, gas lines, steam pipes, telephone lines, fiber optic cable, and electrical power lines, are found in the first 30 feet below street level. Each day 1.2 billion gallons of water flow into New York City from the north. There are more than 80,000 miles of cable under the streets to keep the bright lights in the big city.

Farther down, between 30 and 200 feet below, the subways and the sewers are found. In 1935, the *New York Times* reported that an alligator had been found in one of the sewers! But in general they are considered among the cleanest in the world.

Hundreds of feet below, workers called sandhogs are building the deepest project yet: a giant new water tunnel.

When the circus comes to New York, the elephants walk through the Lincoln Tunnel, the world's only three-tube tunnel.

But it's not all work and no play underground. Many stores, restaurants, movie theaters, and music clubs are located below street level. The Village Vanguard, one of the most famous jazz clubs in the world, opened in 1935 in a basement in Greenwich Village, and it is still there, drawing crowds and jazz legends.

A well-loved city landmark, the Oyster Bar, is found on the lower level of Grand Central Terminal. Underneath its tiled ceilings, commuters and locals enjoy seafood as the trains carry more people in and out of New York, to work and to play, above or underground.

the
E N D

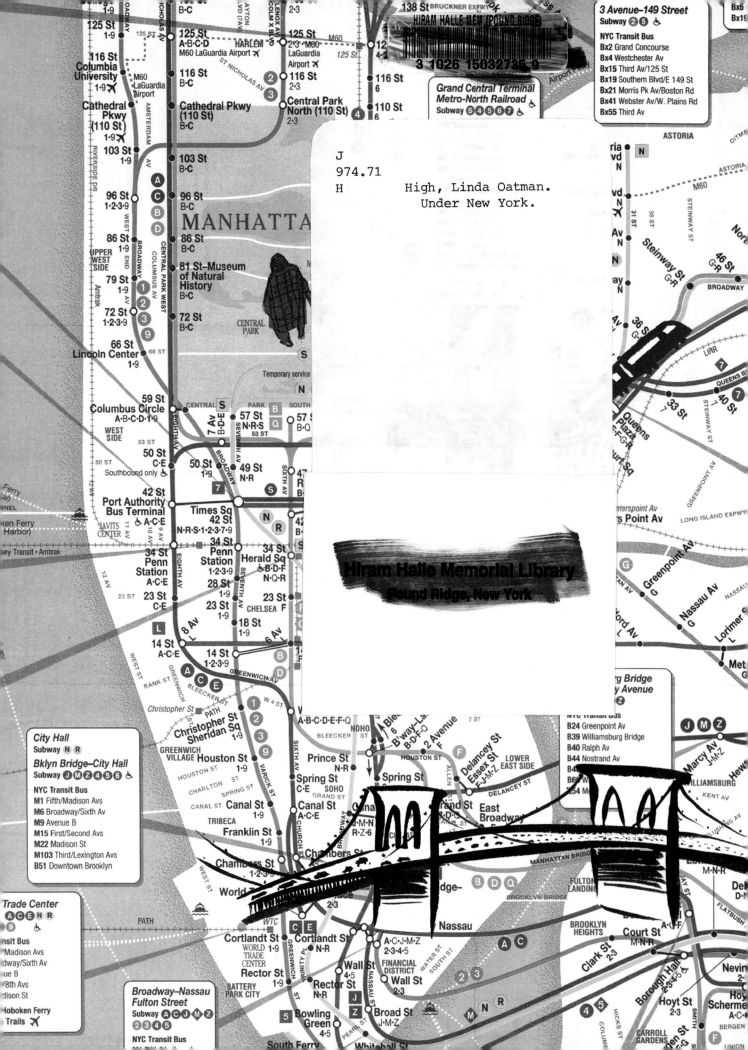